The Stanley CUP

All About Pro Hockey's Biggest Event

by Martin Gitlin

CAPSTONE PRESS

a capstone imprint

Sports Illustrated Kids Winner Takes All is published by Capstone Press,
1710 Roe Crest Drive, North Mankato, Minnesota 56003.
www.capstonepub.com

SI Kids is a trademark of Time Inc. Used with permission.

Library of Congress Cataloging-in-Publication Data
Gitlin, Marty.
    The Stanley Cup : all about pro hockey's biggest event / by Martin Gitlin.
    p. cm.—(Sports illustrated KIDS. Winner takes all.)
    Includes bibliographical references and index.
    Summary: "Describes the NHL's Stanley Cup championship series, including some of
the greatest teams, players, and moments from Stanley Cup history"—Provided by publisher.
    ISBN 978-1-4296-6575-9 (library binding)
    ISBN 978-1-4296-9440-7 (paperback)
    1. Stanley Cup (Hockey)—History—Juvenile literature. I. Title.
GV847.7.G58 2013
796.962648—dc23   2011048855

Editorial Credits
Aaron Sautter, editor; Kazuko Collins, designer; Eric Gohl,
    media researcher; Laura Manthe, production specialist

Photo Credits
123RF: Rocco Macri, cover, 1 (trophy); Corbis: Bettmann,
17; Getty Images: Bruce Bennett Studios, 7, 23; Newscom:
Reuters/Mark Blinch, 5, Reuters/STR, 29; NY Daily News
Archive via Getty Images: Keith Torrie, 25; Sports Illustrated:
David E. Klutho, cover (middle & right), 2–3, 8, 19, 21, 27,
28, Heinz Kluetmeier, 15, Hy Peskin, 9, 10, 11, 18, John
D. Hanlon, 20, John Iacono, 13, Manny Millan, 12 (front),
Robert Beck, cover (background), 26, Tony Triolo, cover (left)

Design Elements
Shutterstock: MaxyM, Redshinestudio, rendergold

Records listed in this book are current as of the 2010–11 season.

Printed in the United States of America in Stevens Point, Wisconsin.
042012   006678WZF12

· TABLE OF CONTENTS ·

Competing for the Cup

The 2009 Stanley Cup Finals between the Pittsburgh Penguins and Detroit Red Wings had reached Game 7. With the score tied 0-0 in the second period, the Penguins' Maxime Talbot grabbed the puck near the Red Wings' goal. He squeezed the puck past a defender and the goalie to score.

But the Penguins didn't celebrate for long. Soon after the goal, Sidney Crosby injured his knee. With their star player out of the game, the Penguins looked for another player to step up. Halfway through the second period, Talbot struck again on a 2-on-1 fast break.

Talbot had already become an unlikely hero in the National Hockey League (NHL) playoffs. Most people didn't consider him an offensive threat. He had scored just 12 goals in the entire regular season. But Talbot stunned the hockey world by exploding for seven goals during the playoffs. And he had just given the Penguins a 2-0 lead.

The Red Wings didn't give up. They scored a goal with about six minutes to go in the game. But Talbot's two goals were too much to overcome. The Penguins held on to become the 2009 Stanley Cup champions.

THE LONGEST GAME

The longest Stanley Cup playoff game took place in 1936. It lasted an amazing six overtimes! The Detroit Red Wings finally beat the Montreal Maroons on a game-winning goal by Mud Bruneteau.

Early History

Stanley Cup championships have been celebrated for nearly 120 years. Lord Stanley, the Governor General of Canada, purchased the trophy for $50 in 1893. He planned to present it to the best amateur hockey club in Canada.

The Stanley Cup soon became the trophy teams played for in the "Challenge Cup Era." From 1893 to 1913, Canadian hockey clubs like the Montreal Victorias, Ottawa Silver Seven, and Quebec Bulldogs challenged each other to determine the Stanley Cup champion.

Then from 1914 to 1917, the champions of the Pacific Coast Hockey Association (PCHA) and National Hockey Association (NHA) played for the Stanley Cup. But during these years, many of the NHA's top players left to fight in World War I (1914–1918). With a lack of quality players, the NHA broke apart in 1917.

Several NHA **franchise** owners soon formed the National Hockey League. The league named the annual championship the Stanley Cup Finals. The Cup itself became the prize for winning the title.

franchise—a team that operates under the rules and regulations of a professional sports league or organization

The Montreal Amateur Athletics Association won the first Stanley Cup title in 1893.

Today 30 NHL teams start each season with the dream of winning the Stanley Cup. The teams are split into the Eastern Conference and Western Conference. Each conference has three divisions of five teams. Teams play 82 games during the regular season. They receive two points for each victory. If they lose they get zero points. If a team loses in overtime or in a **shootout** loss, they receive one point. Overtimes and shootouts are played when teams end three regular periods of play in a tie.

shootout—a method of breaking a tie score at the end of an overtime period

The top eight teams in each conference reach the playoffs. The division winners are given the top three **seeds**. The other teams are seeded four through eight, based on the point totals from their regular season records.

Each playoff round consists of a best-of-seven series. The teams battle through three rounds of playoffs to determine the Eastern and Western conference winners. The conference champions then play each other in the Stanley Cup Finals. The first team to win four games in the Finals series is declared the NHL champion.

Jacques Plante

NAME MISTAKES

Every year, the Stanley Cup trophy is engraved with the names of each player on the championship team. But names are sometimes misspelled. Legendary goaltender Jacques Plante won six Stanley Cup titles with the Montreal Canadiens. His name is misspelled five times on the Cup.

seed—how a team is ranked for the playoffs based on its regular season record and point total

GREATEST DYNASTIES

Throughout Stanley Cup history, several teams have been powerhouses. They've played in many championship series and have come away with several titles. But a few teams have risen even higher to become true **dynasties** in the league.

Canada in Command

From 1942 through most of the 1960s, the Stanley Cup rarely traveled outside of Canada. The Montreal Canadiens and Toronto Maple Leafs dominated the Cup. The Canadiens won 18 titles from 1944 to 1979. During those 36 seasons, Montreal reached the finals an amazing 24 times. When the Canadiens didn't win the Stanley Cup, the Maple Leafs usually did. The team captured six out of 10 titles from 1942 to 1951. Toronto went on to win four more championships between 1962 and 1967.

Montreal Canadiens wing
Maurice "Rocket" Richard

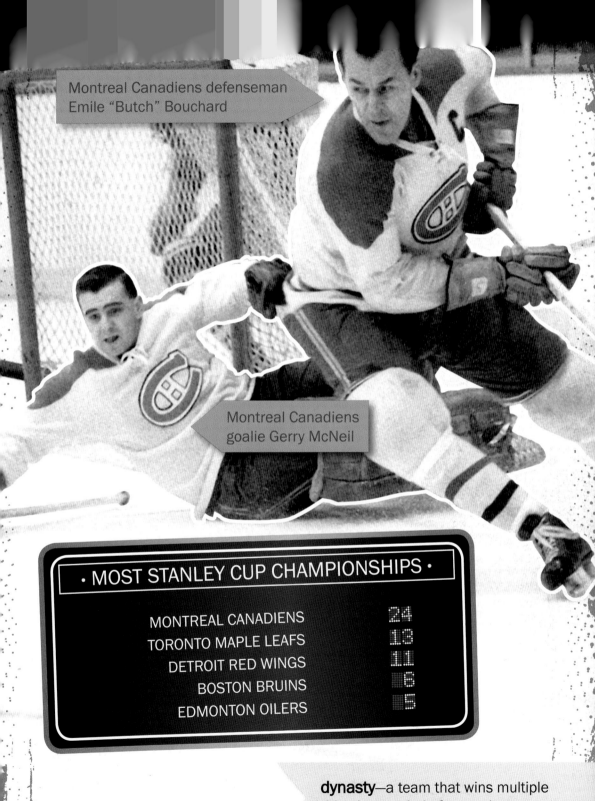

Montreal Canadiens defenseman Emile "Butch" Bouchard

Montreal Canadiens goalie Gerry McNeil

· MOST STANLEY CUP CHAMPIONSHIPS ·

MONTREAL CANADIENS	24
TORONTO MAPLE LEAFS	13
DETROIT RED WINGS	11
BOSTON BRUINS	6
EDMONTON OILERS	5

dynasty—a team that wins multiple titles in a period of several years

Super Islanders

The NHL began adding teams and expanded rapidly in the late 1960s. It soon became nearly impossible for one team to dominate the Stanley Cup. One exception was the New York Islanders, the first U.S. team to enjoy a dynasty.

The Islanders first entered the league in 1972. They snagged their first Stanley Cup just eight years later in 1980. The team went on to win three more championships from 1981 to 1983.

The Islanders featured several future NHL Hall of Famers, including Mike Bossy and Bryan Trottier. During their four-year dynasty, the Islanders compiled an incredible 16-3 record in the Stanley Cup Finals. During the 1982 and 1983 finals, they never lost a game.

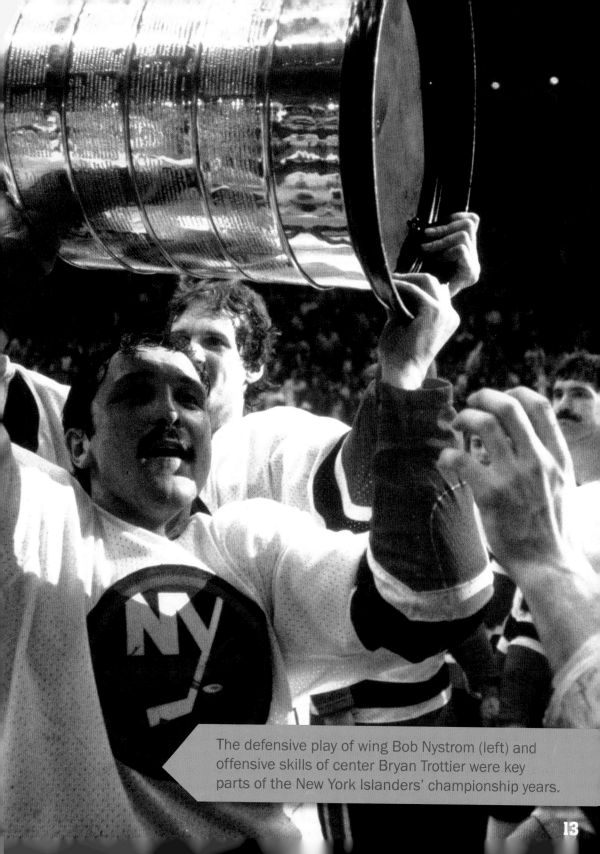

The defensive play of wing Bob Nystrom (left) and offensive skills of center Bryan Trottier were key parts of the New York Islanders' championship years.

Overpowering Oilers

The Islanders' dynasty ended just as the Edmonton Oilers began their own. Some believe the Oilers were the most explosive team in NHL history. The team began showing their dominance in 1984. They overpowered their opponents while averaging a league-record 5.58 goals per game. They won the Stanley Cup that year, and again in 1985, 1987, 1988, and 1990.

The Oilers didn't just steamroll through the regular season and playoffs every year. They dominated the championship round too. With superstar center Wayne Gretzky leading the way, the Oilers scored an average of 21 goals in all five Stanley Cup titles.

The Oilers defense was also dominant during the team's championship years. Opponents averaged just 2.4 goals per game in those series. In the 1990 finals, the Oilers held the Boston Bruins to just eight goals in five games.

BOSTON SURPRISE

In 1953 the Boston Bruins somehow made it into the playoffs with a losing record. But they still found a way to get past the powerful Detroit Red Wings to play the Montreal Canadiens in the championship series.

Wayne Gretzky won the 1985 Stanley Cup Most Valuable Player (MVP) award while leading Edmonton to its second championship.

GREAT PERFORMANCES

Hockey is a team sport, and it takes a whole team to win a Stanley Cup title. But the greatest players often take control to lead their teams to victory.

Scoring Explosions

Four-game sweeps in the finals are rarely exciting. But Wayne Gretzky made the 1988 finals against Boston one to remember. Gretzky had already been a huge star in the NHL. Many thought he couldn't get any better. But then he surprised even his biggest fans. Gretzky scored 13 points, including 10 assists, that helped his team score goal after goal against the Bruins. Gretzky's amazing play on the ice turned the 1988 Stanley Cup finals into a rout.

Few people thought anyone could match Gretzky on the ice. But then Mario Lemieux came along. In the 1991 Stanley Cup Finals, the Pittsburgh Penguins had lost two of the first three games against the Minnesota North Stars. But then Lemieux caught fire. He scored three goals and added six assists in the last three games. Pittsburgh scored a whopping 19 goals during that three-game stretch to capture the Stanley Cup championship.

Wayne Gretzky

• MOST POINTS SCORED IN A STANLEY CUP FINAL SERIES •

POINTS	PLAYER, TEAM	OPPONENT	YEAR
13	WAYNE GRETZKY, OILERS	BRUINS	1988
12	GORDIE HOWE, RED WINGS	CANADIENS	1955
12	YVAN COURNOYER, CANADIENS	BLACKHAWKS	1973
12	JACQUES LEMAIRE, CANADIENS	BLACKHAWKS	1973
12	MARIO LEMIEUX, PENGUINS	NORTH STARS	1991

Sometimes a hot goaltender can help carry a team to a Stanley Cup title. Terry Sawchuk did just that in 1952. He performed brilliantly as his Detroit Red Wings swept Montreal in the Cup finals. Sawchuk gave up only one goal in each of the first two games. Then he kept the Canadiens out of the net completely in the last two games. Many hockey experts feel Sawchuk's performance was the most dominant in Stanley Cup history.

Terry Sawchuk

In 2001 the New Jersey Devils experienced a similar defeat. They were blanked twice against sizzling Colorado Avalanche goaltender Patrick Roy. The Devils won three of the first five games in the series. But then Roy slammed the door shut. In Game 6 he allowed New Jersey to score just once. Then he finished the series in style by shutting out the Devils in Game 7.

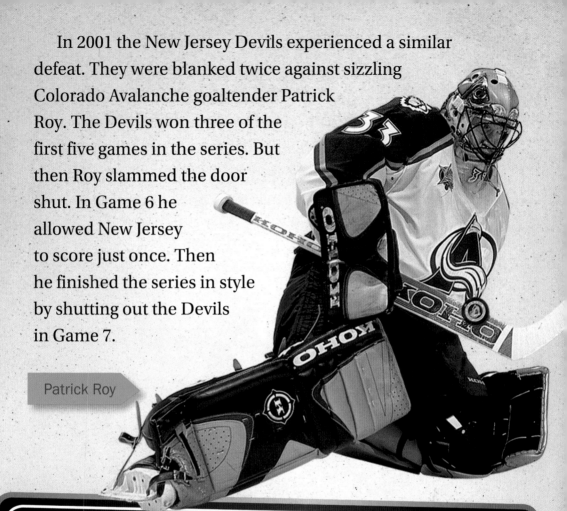

Patrick Roy

· MOST CAREER WINS BY A GOALTENDER ·
IN STANLEY CUP FINALS

WINS	PLAYER, TEAM
31	TURK BRODA, MAPLE LEAFS
25	JACQUES PLANTE, CANADIENS
24	KEN DRYDEN, CANADIENS
19	TERRY SAWCHUK, RED WINGS/MAPLE LEAFS
18	PATRICK ROY, CANADIENS/AVALANCHE

DYNAMITE DEFENDERS

For many years, the job of an NHL **defenseman** was to prevent the opposing team from scoring. But that was before Boston's Bobby Orr came along. He helped redefine the position by becoming a productive scorer, as well as a strong defender.

Orr's fantastic play led the Bruins to sweep the St. Louis Blues in the 1970 championship. They had beaten St. Louis in the first three games, but the Blues refused to quit. They battled Boston into overtime in Game 4. Orr scored the game winner that clinched the Cup. It also helped him earn MVP honors for the series.

Bobby Orr

A RUSSIAN VISIT

The Stanley Cup trophy traveled to Russia for the first time in 1997. It was brought there by several Russian players who played for the Detroit Red Wings.

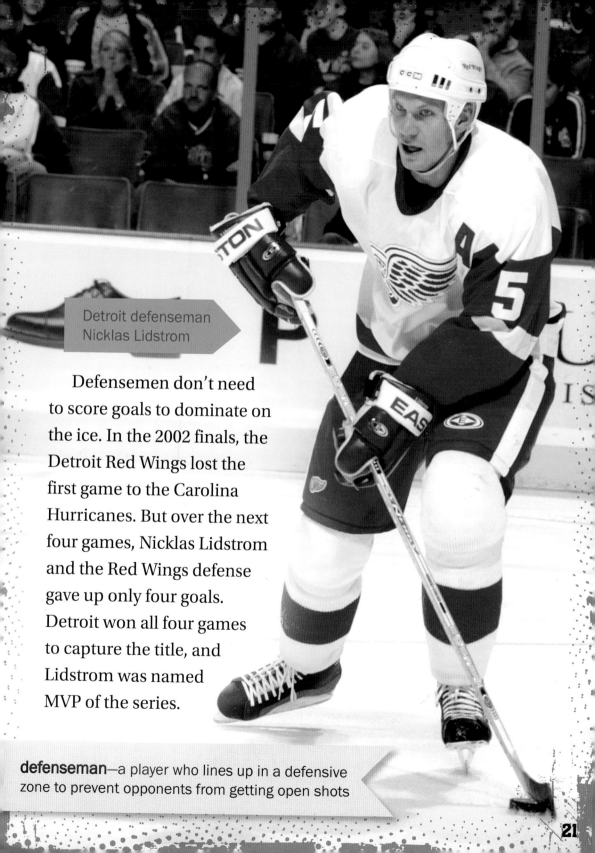

Detroit defenseman Nicklas Lidstrom

Defensemen don't need to score goals to dominate on the ice. In the 2002 finals, the Detroit Red Wings lost the first game to the Carolina Hurricanes. But over the next four games, Nicklas Lidstrom and the Red Wings defense gave up only four goals. Detroit won all four games to capture the title, and Lidstrom was named MVP of the series.

defenseman—a player who lines up in a defensive zone to prevent opponents from getting open shots

AMAZING MOMENTS

The Stanley Cup finals are often filled with excitement and drama. Over the years, the finals have had some historic moments.

1987 – Edmonton vs. Philadelphia

In the 1986–87 season, the Philadelphia Flyers had the second-best defense in the NHL. The Edmonton Oilers had the NHL's finest offense. It was only a matter of time before the two teams battled for the Stanley Cup championship.

Edmonton won three of the first four games, and Oilers fans were already boasting about a victory parade. But the Flyers showed their talent and guts. The team fell behind by two goals in both Games 5 and 6. But they stormed back to win both games and force a Game 7.

However, Edmonton proved to be too strong of a team. Goaltender Grant Fuhr shut down the Flyers in a 3-1 victory in Game 7. The Oilers won their third championship in four years, and the fans got to enjoy their victory parade.

The Oilers' Mark Messier (left) and the Flyers' Dave Poulin battled to control the puck during Game 3 of the 1987 Stanley Cup Finals.

1942 – Toronto vs. Detroit

The Toronto Maple Leafs appeared doomed in the 1942 Stanley Cup Finals. They lost the first two games at home against the Detroit Red Wings. Then they lost Game 3 in Detroit as well.

Toronto coach Hap Day decided to take drastic action. He benched several veteran players and replaced them with **rookies**. Led by future Hall of Famer Syl Apps, the Leafs responded with three straight wins to force the first Game 7 in history. In the final game, Toronto's goaltender Turk Broda kept the Red Wings to just one goal. The Leafs won the final game 3-1 to achieve possibly the greatest comeback in NHL history.

1994 – Vancouver vs. New York

The last time the New York Rangers had won the Stanley Cup, the NHL had just six teams. But the Rangers' fortunes were about to change in the 1994 Stanley Cup Finals. The Rangers won three of the first four games against the Vancouver Canucks. New York was on the brink of winning its first championship in 54 years. But the Canucks stormed back to tie the series.

rookie—a first-year player

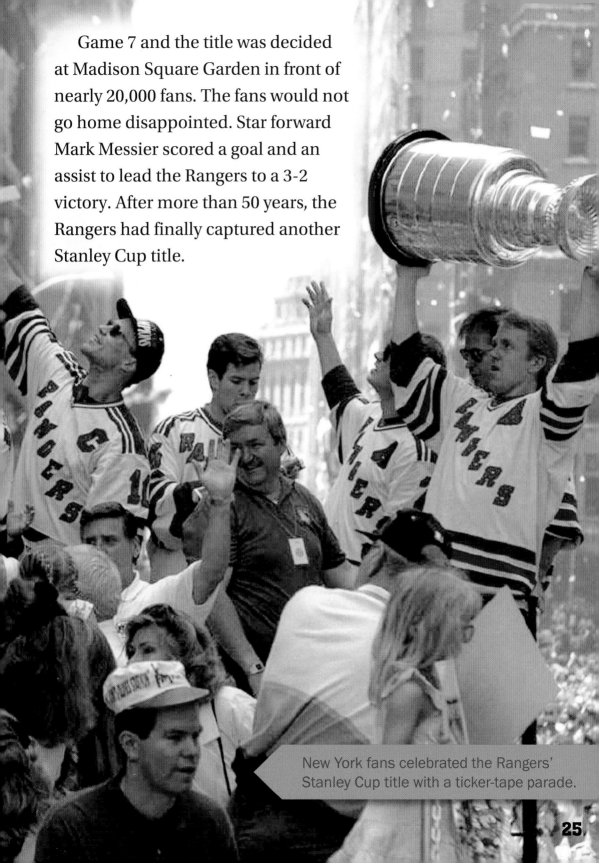

Game 7 and the title was decided at Madison Square Garden in front of nearly 20,000 fans. The fans would not go home disappointed. Star forward Mark Messier scored a goal and an assist to lead the Rangers to a 3-2 victory. After more than 50 years, the Rangers had finally captured another Stanley Cup title.

New York fans celebrated the Rangers' Stanley Cup title with a ticker-tape parade.

Boston Bruins wing
Michael Ryder

Vancouver Canucks
goalie Roberto Luongo

The Boston Bruins' dominating offensive play took the Vancouver
Canucks by surprise in the 2011 Stanley Cup Finals.

LOPSIDED SHOCKER

The Vancouver Canucks were expected to win it all in 2011. The team had the most explosive offense and the strongest defense in the NHL. Vancouver had won eight of 11 games leading up to the championship round.

But the Canucks seemed outmatched by Boston in the 2011 Stanley Cup series. Vancouver earned a narrow 1-0 victory in the first game of the series. Game 2 went to overtime, which the Canucks also won 3-2. But then the Bruins turned up the heat. Boston's offense exploded to score 21 goals over the five games and claim the title. Meanwhile, the Canucks managed to score only four goals. Although they were favored to win the championship, Vancouver couldn't overcome Boston's powerful offense. Boston finished the series with 15 more goals than Vancouver. The Canucks set a record low by scoring just eight goals in seven games. It was the most lopsided score ever seen in a seven-game Stanley Cup series.

Boston Bruins defenseman Zdeno Chara

FUN WITH THE CUP

The Stanley Cup is about 35 inches (89 centimeters) tall and weighs about 35 pounds (16 kilograms). And it keeps getting bigger. More rings are added to the base as it is filled with the names of winning players.

The Cup is a unique trophy. The players and employees of the winning team each get to keep the Cup for one day. If it could talk, it would have some wild stories to tell. Over the years the Cup has been used as everything from a flowerpot to a soup bowl. It has been used to baptize babies. And some players have allowed their pets to drink out of it!

In 1924 some Montreal Canadiens players were on their way to a victory party when their car got a flat tire. They took the Cup out of the trunk to get the spare tire. But when they left, they forgot the trophy in a snowbank on the side of the road! Luckily, they soon realized it was missing. When they drove back, it was sitting right where they had left it.

ONE WEIRD CUSTOM

One of the strangest traditions in the NHL takes place in Detroit. Red Wings fans sometimes throw octopuses onto the ice! Two Detroit storeowners started the tradition during the playoffs in 1952. At that time, it took eight victories to win the Stanley Cup. Each tentacle of the octopus represented a playoff win.

During a trip to his home country of Slovakia, Detroit's Tomas Kopecky ate tripe soup out of the Stanley Cup!

GLOSSARY

center (SEN-tur)—the player who participates in a face-off at the beginning of play

defenseman (dih-FENS-muhn)—a player who lines up in a defensive zone to prevent opponents from getting open shots on goal

dynasty (DYE-nuh-stee)—a team that wins multiple championships in a period of several years

franchise (FRAN-chize)— a team that operates under the rules and regulations of a professional sports league or organization

overtime (OH-vur-time)—an extra period played if the score is tied at the end of a game

rookie (RUK-ee)—a first-year player

seed (SEED)—how a team is ranked for the Stanley Cup playoffs, based on the team's regular season record and point total

shootout (SHOOT-out)—a method of breaking a tie score at the end of overtime play

READ MORE

Frederick, Shane. *The Ultimate Guide to Pro Hockey Teams.* Ultimate Pro Team Guides. Mankato, Minn.: Capstone Press, 2011.

Thomas, Keltie. *Inside Hockey! The Legends, Facts, and Feats That Made the Game.* Toronto: Maple Tree Press, 2008.

Wiseman, Blaine. *Hockey.* Record Breakers. New York: AV2, 2011.

INTERNET SITES

FactHound offers a safe, fun way to find Internet sites related to this book. All of the sites on FactHound have been researched by our staff.

Here's all you do:

Visit *www.facthound.com*

Type in this code: 9781429665759

INDEX